This Journal Belongs to:

morning
B.R.E.W.
journal

You Are a Dancing SPIRIT
Psalm 150:4

Hug Your Blessings
Hebrews 6:14

Give Your Dreams a Standing Ovation
Acts 2:17

Trust Your Way Through
Proverbs 3:5-6

morning
B.R.E.W.
A Divine Power Drink for Your Soul

Be Still
Receive God's Love
Embrace Personhood
Welcome the Day

To order the book and journal containing these empowerment cards visit **www.augsburgfortress.org**

morning
B.R.E.W.
A Divine Power Drink for Your Soul

Be Still
Receive God's Love
Embrace Personhood
Welcome the Day

To order the book and journal containing these empowerment cards visit **www.augsburgfortress.org**

morning
B.R.E.W.
A Divine Power Drink for Your Soul

Be Still
Receive God's Love
Embrace Personhood
Welcome the Day

To order the book and journal containing these empowerment cards visit **www.augsburgfortress.org**

morning
B.R.E.W.
A Divine Power Drink for Your Soul

Be Still
Receive God's Love
Embrace Personhood
Welcome the Day

To order the book and journal containing these empowerment cards visit **www.augsburgfortress.org**

**Think
Triumphant
THOUGHTS**
Proverbs 23:7

**Don't Quit
Before
the
Miracle**
Philippians 3:14

**Trust Your
DREAMS**
Genesis 28:12

**Don't Be
Afraid
of Your
LIGHT**
Matthew 5:14

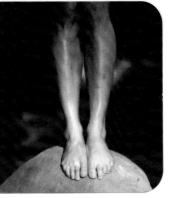

morning

B.R.E.W.

A Divine Power Drink for Your Soul

Be Still
Receive God's Love
Embrace Personhood
Welcome the Day

To order the book and journal containing these empowerment cards visit **www.augsburgfortress.org**

morning

B.R.E.W.

A Divine Power Drink for Your Soul

Be Still
Receive God's Love
Embrace Personhood
Welcome the Day

To order the book and journal containing these empowerment cards visit **www.augsburgfortress.org**

morning

B.R.E.W.

A Divine Power Drink for Your Soul

Be Still
Receive God's Love
Embrace Personhood
Welcome the Day

To order the book and journal containing these empowerment cards visit **www.augsburgfortress.org**

morning

B.R.E.W.

A Divine Power Drink for Your Soul

Be Still
Receive God's Love
Embrace Personhood
Welcome the Day

To order the book and journal containing these empowerment cards visit **www.augsburgfortress.org**

with Empowerment Cards

Kirk Byron Jones

Augsburg Books
MINNEAPOLIS

MORNING B.R.E.W. JOURNAL

Large-quantity purchases or custom editions of this book are available at a discount from the publisher. For more information, contact the sales department at Augsburg Fortress, Publishers, P.O. Box 1209, Minneapolis, MN 55440-1209.

Scripture quotations are from the New Revised Standard Version Bible, copyright © 1989 by the Division of Christian Education of the National Council of the Churches of Christ in the USA and used by permission.

Cover design by Laurie Ingram; cover art © Illustration Works. Used by permission. Book design by Michelle L. N. Cook

ISBN 0-8066-5143-1

The paper used in this publication meets the minimum requirements of American National Standard for Information Sciences—Permanence of Paper for Printed Library Materials, ANSI Z329.48-1985. ♾™

Manufactured in Canada

09   08   07   06   05   1   2   3   4   5   6   7   8   9   10

How to Use Your B.R.E.W. Journal

Thank you for purchasing *Morning B.R.E.W.: A Divine Power Drink for Your Soul* and this accompanying journal. I hope your experience with this simple yet potent devotional discipline will be rewarding.

This journal is not *my* book; it is *your* book. I hope you record your name on the front page and claim this book as your own. This journal is designed to extend and enhance your reflections during your morning B.R.E.W. discipline and to allow you to record your experiences. Alternatively, you could use this book apart from your regular B.R.E.W. time, as a respite in the midst of a busy life or at the end of the day. In addition to giving you traditional journal writing space, I have provided blank space for writing or drawing more creatively, along with some quotes and B.R.E.W. exercises for those who want suggestions for reflection. You probably also noticed the full-color "empowerment cards" when you opened up the journal. These punch-out cards allow you to carry an inspirational thought with you to reflect on throughout the day. I'll explain more about these cards in a moment.

B.R.E.W. is what you make it. Dare to make it faithful, meaningful, and no less important, fun. *Be still; Receive God's love; Embrace your personhood;* and *Welcome the day*, all in a spirit of joyful trusting, wide-eyed openness, and sacred adventure—see the whole matter as *holy play*.

Journal Starters

"But what would I write down?" Sometimes a blank journal page can be intimidating. Have courage! Don't be afraid to speak your unique language, write in your truest voice, and express your most daring thoughts. Here are some strategies to jump-start your pen or pencil:

1. Reflect on your experience in each stage of your daily B.R.E.W. time—or focus on the portion that was most meaningful that day. You might use one or all of the following sentence starters:
- In the *stillness*, I felt/saw:
- While *receiving God's love*, I envisioned/experienced:
- While *embracing my personhood*, I remembered/realized:
- As I *welcomed the day*, I imagined/noticed:

2. Consider the experience wholistically. Are there themes that connect all of the B.R.E.W. phases? What is this telling you? Here's a sentence starter for this type of reflection:
- I feel my B.R.E.W. experience challenging me to change/focus on/risk the following:

3. Reflect on how the B.R.E.W. discipline is contributing to your spiritual, emotional, physical, and social development.
- Spiritually, B.R.E.W. is helping me:
- Emotionally, B.R.E.W. is helping me:
- Physically, B.R.E.W. makes me feel:
- Socially, B.R.E.W. is helping me:

4. Review the "B.R.E.W. Starter" reflection on the left page of each spread. We've included fifty-two reflections in this journal. While you may start the journal at any time of year, please note that the reflections for weeks forty-nine to fifty-one relate to the Christmas season.

5. Don't just record your thoughts—use your imagination! We've given you some blank space on every spread for free-form creativity. In addition, feel free to write on, between, and around the lines and in the margins. Express yourself in a multitude of ways:
- Sketch, doodle, and color
- Write poems, prose, and lyrics

• Create a collage or scrapbook of images or memorabilia that remind you of your B.R.E.W. experience

6. Leave some space for what you know but can't (at least in the moment of your reflection) put into words.

7. Ask questions! Don't be afraid to not answer them right away. Mark them for a second appointment, a return engagement. Your questions will cultivate a greater clarity and focus.

Empowerment Cards

Through God's grace, we co-create our lives through our thoughts, feelings, and actions. Becoming more intentional about what you think is a powerful way to immediately change your life for the better. Jesus's mission, in part, was and is to change the way we think and believe so that we can live more deliberately and joyfully as the children of God we are.

The B.R.E.W. empowerment cards provided in the front and back of this book contain thoughts and ideas to help you live your best life possible. Don't just read them; repeat them, internalize them, make them your own. Let them inspire you to create your own liberating phrases and sentences.

If an empowerment card speaks to you, share it with others as well! Here are several ideas for using the cards to inspire others:
• Leave B.R.E.W. cards in places where someone might read them, such as in coffee shops or on community bulletin boards.
• Drop a B.R.E.W. card in a letter to someone who could use an uplifting message.
• E-mail B.R.E.W. inspirations to friends and family.
• Add B.R.E.W. sayings to your e-mail signature.
• Refer to B.R.E.W. expressions in church newsletters, speeches, and sermons.

Date: _____

Week 1

You can do what can't be done.

B.R.E.W. Starter:
A voice whispered to me one morning,
"Come, let me show you
how to walk on water."

First, one step,
then another,
then a third, imagined.

"You see," said my teacher,
"It's not about what's under your feet;
it's about what's in your heart."
—K.B.J.

Think of a dream or aspiration that continues to tease and taunt you. You may have given up on it, but it has not given up on you. What small things can you do to bring to life something that only seems impossible?

Date: _____

Week 2

"Do you want to be made well?"
—John 5:6

B.R.E.W. Starter: Jesus asked this question of a man who had been sick for thirty-eight years. On the surface, it seems a bit thoughtless: Who doesn't want to be well? Yet in asking, Jesus used the question as a "thought-catcher." To answer the question, the man has to trace his desires about wellness and wholeness.

Whatever your desires and destinations in life, you can be assured of this: your thoughts will either urge you onward or block your path. Identifying, observing, and regulating what we think can become a "make or break"—or even a "life or death"—matter.

What is your answer to Jesus's question, "Do you want to be made well?"

Date: _____

Week 3

"If you do not doubt in your heart, but believe that what you say will come to pass, it will be done for you."
—Mark 11:23

B.R.E.W. Starter: Consider the difference between thoughts and beliefs. Etymologically, *thought* is defined as a mental image, but the word *belief* is linked to love. I look at it this way: *Thoughts are the things we hold in our heads; beliefs are things we hold in our hearts. Believing is the action of breathing our love, our spirit, into our thinking.*

God has decreed thoughts and beliefs to be the basic ingredients with which we join God in co-creating our lives. Pay attention to the first thoughts that enter your mind after *being still*. Do they lift you up or drag you down? How can you encourage your beliefs to grow into your thoughts?

Date: _____

Week 4

"Joy comes with the morning."
—Psalm 30:5

B.R.E.W. Starter: What do you usually wake up thinking? A few years ago, I made a conscious effort to stop thinking about "stuff" first thing in the morning—stuff I had to do, stuff I wanted to do, other people's stuff. If we're not careful, we can be overwhelmed with stuff before we notice the light of day. When you wake up, try "catching the stuff" and holding it at bay until you have had time to bless the day.

Reflect back on your waking moments this week. What stuff-thoughts tried to converge on you right away? How would holding back the stuff help you to better receive and engage the day?

Date: _____

Week 5

"So if anyone is in Christ, there is a new creation: everything old has passed away; see, everything has become new!"
—2 Corinthians 5:17

B.R.E.W. Starter: Do you recall the story I told in *Morning B.R.E.W.* about our young son's morning call, "I waked up"? The essence of his exclamation can be defined using several other words that begin with "ex": *excitement, expectation, exploration,* and *exuberance.* "Ex-" simply means "out." Each new day calls to us, "Come out!" Listen and you will hear it. How do we come out? By receiving each day as an amazing gift of new existence.

What do the "ex-" words mean to you? Think of ways you can cultivate these "ex-" factors.

_____

_____

_____

_____

_____

_____

_____

_____

_____

_____

_____

_____

_____

_____

_____

_____

_____

_____

Date: _____

Week 6

How ready are you to think of something unfamiliar?

B.R.E.W. Starter: In his book, *Awareness*, Anthony de Mello offers some powerful insights on spirituality, what he considers "waking up" your conscience in the deepest, richest way possible. He asserts, "the one thing you need most of all is the readiness to learn something new. The chances that you will 'wake up' are in direct proportion to the amount of truth you can take without running away."

Date: _____

Week 7

"But those who wait for the Lord shall renew their strength, they shall mount up with wings like eagles, they shall run and not be weary, they shall walk and not faint."
—Isaiah 40:31

B.R.E.W. Starter: B.R.E.W. is a way of waiting on or sitting with God. Isaiah says that when we choose to do this, we can expect God to rub off on us in three distinct ways. We will find ourselves filled with the strength of exuberance, feeling at times like we can do anything in the world. I call this soaring strength. Second, we will feel new energy to engage everyday tasks with attentiveness and vigor. This is the strength of activism. Then there is the strength "to walk and not faint." This is the strength to hold on when the going gets tough. This is the strength of enlightened perseverance.

Think of moments when you have felt each type of strength. What strength do you need the most now?

Date: _____

Week 8

How sweet it is to be loved by God.

B.R.E.W. Starter: Did you have a favorite song when you were growing up? I did, and a few years ago I purchased a CD that included my favorite song, "How Sweet It Is (To Be Loved by You)" by Junior Walker and the All Stars. Something went through me as soon as I heard Walker's saxophone introducing this rhythm and blues classic. This song reminds me that God is the source of all love, and there is no love sweeter than God's love for each one of us.

What songs make you think of God's love? What images capture the experience of receiving God's love?

Date: _____

Week 9

"Enter through the narrow gate; for the gate is wide and the road is easy that leads to destruction, and there are many who take it."
—*Matthew 7:13*

B.R.E.W. Starter: The way that Jesus offers us may be narrow in the sense of difficulty, but it is far from narrow in viewpoint. Jesus opens and widens us with his teachings. Take for instance "love your enemy," and "let your light shine," or "all things are possible." Jesus challenges us to question and, ultimately, evict conventional beliefs, especially those that give us a feeling of power over others. He persistently encourages us to think about life, relationships, and spirituality in more expansive ways.

Which of your viewpoints would Jesus commend? For which points does he invite you to open your thinking and expand your beliefs?

Date: _____

Week 10

God so loves; why don't we?

B.R.E.W. Starter: While many of us may know John 3:16 by heart, I am not sure we have comprehended the "so loved" part. If we did understand, the lavishness of our love for ourselves and each other would show more. I once heard it said that love is spelled "t-i-m-e." This week, consider taking the time that you would use to reflect in this journal and use it instead to be with someone you love. Perhaps the someone who most needs your love and time is you. If that's the case, do something special for yourself this week.

Date: _____

Week 11

"Let no one deceive you with empty words."
—Ephesians 5:6

B.R.E.W. Starter: Richard Bach's *Jonathan Livingston Seagull* is about a seagull that refuses to accept the accepted beliefs about how and where he should fly. Early on in his path to soaring liberation, Jonathan hears a voice of resistance, which he calls "the hollow voice": it is the voice of his own doubts and fears. All of us have a hollow voice, a voice devoid of aspiration that leaves us feeling if not empty, then longing for more. If we are to soar, we must ignore this voice, until the time the hollow voice is silenced altogether.

When are you most likely to hear your hollow voice? What can you do to become better at ignoring it?

Date: _____

Week 12

What are you hiding?

B.R.E.W. Starter: I know a dear soul with a gift for smiling softly and easily, with sparkling eyes. Her delight blesses others. A youngster once asked her why she smiled so. She responded, "I just do." The child then asked, "What are you hiding?" What a question! What was behind it? The child's play of hide-and-seek, secret-holding and secret-telling? Or maybe the joy of surprise? Whatever the reason, he tied smiling to secrecy, to something hidden that came out disguised as a smile.

I imagine God whispering a special secret to each of us at the moment of our birth, something that has the power to make us smile for no apparent reason. What secret did God whisper to you?

Date: _____

Week 13

Let the guilt go. Choose to live in God's grace.

B.R.E.W. Starter: One morning during prayer, I confessed a short-coming and sought God's grace and forgiveness. As my prayer proceeded, I mentioned this fault again and received this response, "I forgave you the first time; I graced you the first time. If I haven't brought it up again, why are you?" Then I looked out the window. Down below was a lake surrounded by trees, which resembled hearts. In that moment, I was surrounded by God's love and wept tears of release.

We sabotage God's grace by clinging to guilt, shame, and remorse. Stop beating yourself up. Whatever the wrong, God's grace saves us. What will it take for God to convince you that you really are forgiven?

Date: _____

Week 14

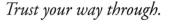

Trust your way through.

B.R.E.W. Starter:

There is meaning in waiting
There will be someone or something
to help you at the trying places on your path
Unseen ground is not unsure ground
Discouragement still has courage in it
There are marvelous hidden lessons in the valley moments
Take strength from struggle
Trust your way through
—K.B.J.

What lessons have you learned in the valley? How has God helped you through?

Date: _____

Week 15

"And you will know the truth, and the truth will make you free."
—John 8:32

B.R.E.W. Starter: The movie *Ray*, about the life of Ray Charles, presents a poignant lesson about facing fear. After the death of her youngest son, Charles's mother stares squarely into Ray's blinded eyes and challenges him to live an adventurous life *in spite of* his blindness. Ray does that, but he is haunted with guilt over his brother's death. Later, when his blindness is lifted momentarily, Ray sees his dead mother and brother offering him sweet grace and courage. In his heart, he sees the loving truth that sets him free from fear.

Stare your trouble in the face until it softens. It just may show you something that will set you free to live your best life.

Date: _____

Week 16

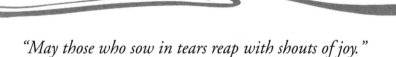

"May those who sow in tears reap with shouts of joy."
—*Psalm 126:5*

B.R.E.W. Starter: The girl's reading about her mother's fight against breast cancer started strong, but soon, overcome by tears, she stopped speaking. She stood alone at the podium with her big burden. Finally, she began again, and her story took a surprising turn. What many of us thought was the story of loss was actually a testimony of triumph. The girl's mother was still alive! Through pain and struggle, assisted by physicians and a loving family, the mother survived. The daughter wasn't crying because things had ended badly; she was crying because things had not ended at all.

Reflect on the sad and glad things that made you cry in the past. What has the power to make you cry now?

Date: _____

Week 17

"Only when it is darkest can you see the stars."
—Martin Luther King Jr.

B.R.E.W. Starter: A young student pinned this description to her painting of a night sky:

> ". . . My favorite part was making the stars. I was trying to make the stars sparkle. Finally, I thought of a way to prick the paint out of the sky (which she had painted black and gray) so that the white posterboard underneath will show."

We are so used to seeing stars that we don't think about our power to create them. We have the power to form fantastic things in our lives if we would only have the imagination and courage to create them.

What wonderful things would you like to see happen? What can you do to make your dreams come true?

Date: _____

Week 18

"You are the light of the world."
—*Matthew 5:14*

B.R.E.W. Starter: Sometimes my B.R.E.W. time coincides with sunrise—not the first moments of faint light on the horizon, but when the sun finally appears as a brilliant ball of light. One morning, I wrote the following words in my journal:

> Bright light of exaltation and expectation
> Behold its glory
> Love and Trust its brilliance
> And your own

Given Jesus's words in John 5:14, the sun sees in us what we see in it. Whenever we observe morning light, it is always a case of light looking at light. What traits and gifts do you have that are especially helpful to others?

Date: _____

Week 19

"I came that they may have life, and have it abundantly."
—*John 10:10*

B.R.E.W. Starter: Many people think about life as being a burdensome affair with rules and responsibilities, hardships and heartaches. They always seem weighted down by living. They have been taught to believe that life is essentially more bitter than sweet.

Now hear this: Feeling downtrodden is not a prerequisite for faithful discipleship; soul-heaviness is no sign of holiness. Cultivate the habit of thinking and feeling alive and free. Live as though you were the child of a wildly wonderful God. The truth is that it wouldn't be make believe. How can you start living life more abundantly?

Date: _____

Week 20

"Take thought for what is noble in the sight of all."
—*Romans 12:17*

B.R.E.W. Starter: When our daughter, Jovonna, was eleven, she couldn't sleep one night because of bad thoughts. In the morning, I showed her a solution over breakfast. I asked Jovonna to think about the sausage we were fixing. She played along. I asked her to think about orange juice instead. After awhile, I asked her turn her thoughts to her plans for the day. To answer her quizzical look, I explained that we have an amazing ability: the power to think—and not to think—about anything we want.

Jesus invites us to think and dream in new, more expansive ways. In what ways do your thoughts encourage or restrict abundant living? What do you want to think about?

Date: _____

Week 21

"Now you, my friends, are children of the promise."
—Galatians 4:28

B.R.E.W. Starter: One of the hardest things of all is deciding God's will in a particular situation. In the article "Honoring Verna Dozier," published in *The Witness Magazine*, Bishop Jane Holmes Dixon writes about the advice she received from this amazing woman. Verna explained, "Every decision has both cost and promise. . . . If the cost outweighs the promise, then you do not take action; if the promise outweighs the cost then you act."[1]

The Bishop then asked her what happens if, after doing that, you still make the wrong decision. "Then you ask God's forgiveness," replied Verna. "You do believe in grace and forgiveness, don't you?"

How do you discern God's will for your life?

---

1. See *www.thewitness.org/agw/dixon081004.html*

Date: _____

Week 22

You were born to soar!

B.R.E.W. Starter: A spiritual teacher tells this story: A farmer put an eagle's egg in a barnyard hen's nest. The eaglet hatched and grew up with the other chicks. He scratched for worms and insects. He clucked and cackled. He thrashed his wings but never flew more than a few feet into the air.

Years passed. One day the old eagle saw a magnificent bird gliding on the wind, with scarcely a beat of its strong wings. "What's that?" he asked. "That's the eagle, the king of the birds," said the other chickens. "He belongs to the sky. We belong to the earth—we're chickens." So the eagle lived and died a chicken, for that's what he thought he was.

What prevents you from living the life you were intended to live?

Date: _____

Week 23

Discover the gift of solitude.

B.R.E.W. Starter: A great actress once revealed her method for getting into character: living in nearly complete solitude. She went out only occasionally to eat and to visit with family. Everyone who saw her stunning performances had to say that her time alone must have been well spent.

Jesus often sought out time alone. One of the greatest things we can give to the world and those we love is our solitude. Solitude allows us the chance to connect with our true selves, our best selves. It allows us to own anew who we are and who we are becoming. Buoyed by time alone, we are refreshed to offer others fresh blessings.

How do you use your solitude?

_____

_____

_____

_____

_____

_____

_____

_____

_____

_____

_____

_____

_____

_____

_____

_____

_____

_____

Date: _____

Week 24

You are a dancing spirit.

B.R.E.W. Starter: In one of my favorite pictures, Dr. Martin Luther King Jr. is dancing with his wife at a ball in Stockholm, Sweden, where he accepted the 1964 Nobel Peace Prize. As a Baptist preacher, Martin normally refused to dance. But he agreed to dance here, and the couple clearly enjoyed it.

In her autobiography, *Dancing Spirit,* the legendary Judith Jamison describes how dancing enlarges your spirit:

> Go into the depths of your heart to pull out what you need to communicate with another person. . . . When you extend your arm, it doesn't stop at the end of your fingers, because you're dancing bigger than that; you're a dancing spirit. . . . Let your light shine.[2]

What makes you feel like a dancing spirit?

2. *Judith Jamison,* Dancing Spirit *(New York: Doubleday, 1993), 234.*

_____

_____

_____

_____

_____

_____

_____

_____

_____

_____

_____

_____

_____

_____

_____

_____

_____

_____

Date: _____

Week 25

Live life at a savoring pace.

B.R.E.W. Starter: To savor is to take pleasure in, to relish, to enjoy. The word's Latin origin—*sapere*—means both "taste" and "be wise." Notice the connection between the physical and the psychological meaning. For me, savoring is the physical slowing as well as the revelation within the slowing. Instead of practicing our frenzied pattern of paying attention to more, savoring pace challenges us to slow down and pay more attention.

You can create a savoring pace. Focus on both ordinary and extraordinary sightings for a few moments longer. Pay attention to sounds *and* silences. Think more deeply by leaning into new experiences (instead of running away). Savoring pace yields a richer, brighter life that opens to us once we slow down enough to notice it. To learn more about living at a savoring pace, visit www.savoringpace.com.

_____

_____

_____

_____

_____

_____

_____

_____

_____

_____

_____

_____

_____

_____

_____

_____

_____

Date: _____

Week 26

"Beloved, let us love one another, because love is from God; everyone who loves is born of God and knows God."
—*1 John 4:7*

B.R.E.W. Starter: I am writing this after listening to a CD featuring Louis Armstrong and Ella Fitzgerald. As far as I am concerned, those two jazz greats are proofs of the existence of God. Their combined contribution is a testimony to layered love. In each selection, I hear them loving the song, loving the act of singing and playing, and loving each other.

This week, you might try an experiment: listen to this duo yourself. Savor their sounds. Then read the book of 1 John. Jot down some reflections on both experiences, including how the listening and reading may have intersected with each other.

Date: _____

Week 27

"Let each of you lead the life that the Lord has assigned, to which God called you."
—1 Corinthians 7:17

B.R.E.W. Starter: We are passing the midway point in the journal. It's a good time to reflect upon where your B.R.E.W. experiences are leading you. Read over what you have written in the weeks past and listen for recurring themes. Do you sense a need to change? Are there challenges that you need to focus on? What risks have you taken? What risks do you have yet to take?

Date: _____

Week 28

X-ray your love.

B.R.E.W. Starter: In his book *The Inner Voice of Love*, the late Henri Nouwen suggests that all that appears to be love is not, that we sometimes give and receive love "more out of need than out of trust." He warns against love that manipulates others—love given in an effort to receive affection or support. It is only when you give and receive love out of trust that "you will be grateful for what is given to you without clinging to it, and joyful for what you can give without bragging about it. You will be a free person, free to love."[3]

Use Nouwen's words to examine your love for others. How can you love more in the best and finest sense of the word?

---

3. *Henri Nouwen,* The Inner Voce of Love *(New York: Doubleday, 1996), 65.*

_____

_____

_____

_____

_____

_____

_____

_____

_____

_____

_____

_____

_____

_____

_____

_____

_____

Date: _____

Week 29

"Blessed are the eyes that see what you see!"
—Luke 10:23

B.R.E.W. Starter: A stranger gave me something I will cherish for the rest of my life. As I was walking toward my church, my path intersected with a rather stately, well-attired African American woman. I slowed, allowed her to pass, and greeted her, "Good morning, how are you? " Her response was immediate and forthright. She proclaimed, "I'm too blessed to complain." The words of this stranger turned a light on, started an engine, lit a fire. The comment put a smile on my face and gave me a new perspective on living that I want to hold on to forever.

What do you complain about during the day? How do your blessings stack up to your complaints? In what ways are troubles blessings?

_____

_____

_____

_____

_____

_____

_____

_____

_____

_____

_____

_____

_____

_____

_____

_____

_____

_____

_____

Date: _____

Week 30

Step into new freedom.

B.R.E.W. Starter: In Philadelphia, I came across a striking sculpture by Zenos Frudakas. In front is a person in open stride, arms outstretched, face turned toward the sky. Behind this person are four vertical tombs. One is empty—the freed soul has just emerged. In the others, three more beings are coming out.

Immediately I marveled, "What a picture of freedom!" Then I saw the writing in the empty tomb where a head once rested: "Stand here." The artist didn't stop at expressing freedom; he wanted viewers to experience it. I walked into the empty space and stood still. Then I took a delightful step into freedom.

Imagine the confinement of a tomb, then the joy as you step out. How can this image help you with your fears?

Date: _____

Week 31

Be prepared to let God's love rain down on you.

B.R.E.W. Starter: One morning, I suddenly felt overcome with a flowing, filling feeling of God's love. The immediacy and visceral manifestation startled me; I didn't just think about something magnificent, I felt something magnificent.

I have physically felt God's love before. On my office window hangs a stained glass picture of a waterfall surrounded by flowers. I often imagine myself in that picture, the downward streaming waters being God's love raining down on me. Yet that experience takes mental focus to create. This time it happened immediately. Being overcome with washing waters of acceptance and grace was deeply moving. I realized I did not have to mentally place myself under God's love to be touched by such love.

Are you ready to receive God's love, in gratitude and delight?

_____

_____

_____

_____

_____

_____

_____

_____

_____

_____

_____

_____

_____

_____

_____

_____

_____

Date: _____

Week 32

Practice holy amnesia.

B.R.E.W. Starter: "Do not remember the former things or consider the things of old" (Isaiah 43:18). These words are particularly noteworthy considering that many of the verses before it talk about remembrance. The beat of chapter 43 is deliberate and steady until verse 18, when for no apparent reason Isaiah strikes a dissonant sound: "Do not remember . . ."

An old newspaper headline gives meaning to Isaiah's strange stroke, declaring "Dead Paid Off by Social Security." The article revealed that $31 million had been paid to deceased beneficiaries who were listed as dead in the agency's own files. Yes, the dead past can have too much influence over the living present.

What aspects of your past keep you from actively and creatively engaging the future?

Date: _____

Week 33

Plan to improvise.

B.R.E.W. Starter: Saxophonist Sonny Rollins is known for his improvisational solos. He explains that he first learns the material, then he tries "to blot out my mind and let it flow by itself. So I try not to really think too much about what I am playing when I am playing."

We often attempt to manage our busy lives by planning out our days from start to finish, dotting every "i" and crossing every "t." While holding to a schedule can lead to accomplishments, it can also cause us to miss the gifted flow of the day, the ways in which life comes to us by itself. Approach your day with alternative rhythms and surprises in mind. Plan to improvise on a moment's notice.

Date: _____

Week 34

Don't fall to all.

B.R.E.W. Starter: Luke 8:40-42 tells the story of Jairus waiting to beg Jesus to come to his house and heal his daughter. But he wasn't the only one wanting a favor. "They were all waiting for him." You bet they were. Jesus had halted a storm and cured a man possessed by demons. Is it any wonder Jesus had trouble being unnoticed?

Many in the crowd had needs. Yet note that though "all" waited for him, Jesus responded to the request of just one, Jairus, whose daughter was deathly ill. Jesus gave himself permission to choose one matter for the moment.

Single-mindedness is an endangered practice. This week, try focusing on one task at a time. How does this make you feel?

Date: _____

Week 35

Cultivate a tender spirit.

B.R.E.W. Starter: If I were developing a job description for living in a world where violence and danger were on the rise, "tender" would not make my list of desirable attributes. On the other hand, *tender*'s original meaning—to stretch, to hold out—does cause me to think twice. Would the violence and danger in our world be lessened by the presence of more people who can stretch past their fears and, with perseverance, work and wait for new ways of seeing, listening, and thinking?

Think of a person with whom you are currently at odds. Picture your mutual antagonism as a block of ice. Now focus on melting the ice with prayers, new understanding, and creative ideas for reconciliation. Cultivate that tender spirit.

_____

_____

_____

_____

_____

_____

_____

_____

_____

_____

_____

_____

_____

_____

_____

_____

_____

_____

Date: _____

Week 36

Just to be is a blessing.
—*Abraham Heschel*

B.R.E.W. Starter: Abraham Heschel would say something like that. After the civil rights march in Selma, Heschel also said, "I felt my legs were praying." Both quotes indicate he was in touch with the sacredness of life.

Often and innocently, we associate blessing with select acquisition and holiness with special ritual, locking us into believing that blessing and holiness are extraordinary, isolated experiences. Conversely, Heschel discerned goodness and "Godness" to be nearby. We do not have to go far to experience deep peace and joy. Being present is sufficient enough holy ground.

Consider calling a few "time-ins" this week—a time of paying focused attention to present reality in the flow of everyday life. Notice the moment more and be grateful.

_____

_____

_____

_____

_____

_____

_____

_____

_____

_____

_____

_____

_____

_____

_____

_____

Date: _____

Week 37

Attend to what is alive inside of you.

B.R.E.W. Starter: The late singer, pianist, and songwriter Donny Hathaway created music that resonates with pathos and passion. It can make you cry, and it can make you shout for joy. Hathaway began singing on stage at the age of three. He felt something wonderfully amazing welling up inside of him. At age six, he told his grandmother, "You should hear the music I'm hearing in my head."

What would have happened if Hathaway had been unable to hear the music? What if he ignored it or paid little attention to it? In order for others to be blessed by his artistry, he had to first honor what was coming to life inside of him.

What's most alive inside of you? How can you pay more attention to it?

Date: _____

Week 38

God loves you madly.

B.R.E.W. Starter: I delivered the following blessing at a seminary's graduation ceremony. Allow me to share the same blessing with you:

May you always remember that you are a child of God.

May you know that you are called to abide beneath the waterfall of God's grace.

May you not only receive God's refreshing acceptance, but also revel in it.

Then, from the overflow of your spiritual delight, may your ministry come out for truth and justice and because you just can't help yourself.

Finally, hold on with sanctified tenacity to the good news that's too good not to be true: God loves us all madly.

Date: _____

Week 39

Bless your boats.

B.R.E.W. Starter: Lucille Clifton's treasured poem "Blessing the Boats" trumpets the value of journey in life. Life is movement—with nourishing respite throughout—from place to place and moment to moment. Places aren't always geographical locations. Some challenging trips transport us from old ideas to new insights, from entrenched allegiances to communities in tender formation. But onward we go, if we are to learn and grow.

The poem invites us to love the journey—the trips we choose to make and even the ones life chooses for us. "Blessing the Boats" also invites us to remember the vessels that transport us—the people, ideas, and organizations that carry us onward "beyond the face of fear."

What boats in your life would you like to bless? Make time this week to do just that.

Date: _____

Week 40

Practice divine curiosity.

B.R.E.W. Starter: In theologian Helmut Thielicke's autobiography *Notes from a Wayfarer,* he said that a key to his spiritual maturity was not only learning to experience the Gospel "without fear," but also with "divine curiosity." We can move past not having to fear the message of salvation to exploring the Gospel while rooted in a deep, abiding spiritual trust. Then we can approach our world with a sacred interest in all of life.

What are you curious about in your life? How does curiosity help us grow spiritually? Author John Steinbeck is reported to have defined genius as "a child chasing a butterfly up a mountain." May you manifest in your work, play, and relationships a child's spirit—the spirit of sustained divine curiosity.

Date: _____

Week 41

Watch heaven rejoice.

B.R.E.W. Starter: Answer each of the questions in the following poem. Imagine yourself at your strongest. With God's blessing and encouragement, live toward that vision.

Can you stand
living in light?
Can you imagine
sustained joy,
sharpened intuition,
and expanded intelligence?

Can you wield
the sword
of your own brilliance?
Answer, "Yes."
And watch heaven rejoice.
—K.B.J.

_____

_____

_____

_____

_____

_____

_____

_____

_____

_____

_____

_____

_____

_____

_____

_____

_____

_____

Date: _____

Week 42

Question why.

B.R.E.W. Starter:
Why shouldn't you
look forward
to each new day,
and live as many days
as you can
with as much
desire, energy, and passion
as you can?

Listen for questions that arise from your B.R.E.W. experience this week.
Ponder the most mysterious and pressing ones.

Date: _____

Week 43

Have an astonishing day!

B.R.E.W. Starter: "You are the light of the world" (Matthew 5:14). "The kingdom of God is within you" (Luke 17:21). "Out of the believer's heart shall flow rivers of living water" (John 7:38).

What made Jesus say such things? Why did Jesus speak of humanity in such fabulous ways? In his book *The Power of Intention*, Wayne Dyer writes, "Change the way you look at things, and the things you look at will change."[4] What if what Jesus said about you is true? Tell me, as *light bearing glory*, should you settle on simply having a "nice" day, or strive for something more? Choose to focus on and manifest more splendid visions of yourself.

---

4. *Wayne Dyer,* The Power of Intention *(Carlsbad, Calif.: Hay House, 2004), 256.*

Date: _____

Week 44

The way up is sometimes down.

B.R.E.W. Starter: The brilliant jazz keyboardist Herbie Hancock once reflected on a period of creative unrest. His sextet was successful, but it became harder to achieve something more. He needed inner renewal: "I didn't want to play the music I had been playing, but I didn't know what music I wanted to play. . . . I wanted to find the answers within myself."

By submerging inside himself, Hancock hoped to more clearly identify the next artistic summit. Sometimes we grasp new heights through journeying inside to find our callings. It is a nonsensical truth: The way up is sometimes down.

Pay attention to the troubled waters inside you. Disturbance is often a sign of new growth aching to be realized in your life. Where are you being led?

Date: _____

Week 45

Know God in new ways.

B.R.E.W. Starter: Take several walks this week. Allow your experience to expand your understanding of God and glory.

We know God when we notice:
our feet touching the ground,
the loving effort reflected in a
  neighbor's garden,
a yellow bike lodged before launch
  between two tree trunks,
leftover debris on a porch:
mundane signs of life, past and
  present,
a woman wiping her windshield, and
  waving good morning,
a person pushing a stroller, and
the wondrous way, no matter what,
  life keeps rolling along.
—K.B.J.

Date: _____

Week 46

Stop the self-violence.

B.R.E.W. Starter: Well-meaning people sometimes do themselves in the name of good and God. Through the quick pace and pressures of life, we can become carried away with work, give in to too many demands, take on too many projects, try to help everyone with everything. Thomas Merton identifies this as innate violence: "The frenzy of our activism neutralizes our work for peace. It destroys our inner capacity for peace. It destroys the fullness of our own work, because it kills the root of inner wisdom which makes work fruitful."[5]

Think of things you can do to take better care of yourself. God does not need your exhaustion. There is nothing redemptive about unnecessary suffering.

---

5. *As quoted in Wayne Muller,* Sabbath *(New York: Bantam Books, 1999), 3.*

Date: _____

Week 47

Embrace the freedom.

B.R.E.W. Starter: Imagine that you received the following letter from God:

Dear Child: Although you are an adult, from this day forward, I want you to do everything I tell you to do. I will make all of your decisions for you. I will solve your problems; I will tell you what to do, when to do it, and how. Your job is to do as I say and trust that living this way is in your best interest.
  With Deepest Love,
  Your Divine Parent

How would you react? The truth is that God frees us all to be as purposeful about our lives as we can. So get with it, make some decisions; trust that God is with you.

Date: _____

Week 48

Be surprised by God.

B.R.E.W. Starter: How would we want to meet God? Most of us would want to be prepared, pick the perfect place and time, have written out the perfect thing to say, invite the perfect people to make it the perfect event. Gene Bartlett paints a more realistic picture, however:

> God has an uncanny way of taking care of . . . entrances. While we wait at the airport, as it were, with a representative committee of dignitaries, . . . God has a way of quietly arriving at the bus station, walking up the side street, and slipping, unnoticed, through the servant's chambers.[6]

What have been some of the biggest surprises of your life? Are you ready to be surprised by God?

6. *Gene E. Bartlett,* Postscript to Preaching *(Valley Forge, Penn.: Judson Press, 1981), 80.*

Date: _____

Week 49

Don't run by your blessings.

B.R.E.W. Starter: Holiday preparations can be nightmarish if we allow them to get out of hand. Here are four suggestions:

1. Begin at a place of peace. Start your day with prayer, meditation, inspirational reading, or journaling.

2. Limit multitasking, as you run the risk of not doing either task very well. To save time, share shopping and party planning with family, friends, and coworkers.

3. Resist rushing. Slow down when you feel yourself moving too fast. Make margins in your day for playing, reflecting, and resting.

4. Share quality time with loved ones. It is possible to miss the present joy in pursuit of the next thrill. Maybe the best gift you can give someone this year is more of you.

_____

_____

_____

_____

_____

_____

_____

_____

_____

_____

_____

_____

_____

_____

_____

_____

_____

_____

_____

Date: _____

Week 50

Don't sleepwalk through Christmas.

B.R.E.W. Starter: Have you ever seen someone sleepwalk? They may appear to be awake, but they are in their own world, dealing with their own inner conflict or emotions, oblivious to their surroundings and hazards such as stairs and furniture.

Aside from physically walking in our sleep, there are other ways we can sleepwalk. We can repress our feelings about social justice or blind ourselves to problems in our relationships. We can even sleepwalk through our spiritual reflection and worship, even Christmas. We may appear to be awake at Christmas through our apparent activity, but we might actually be asleep to the crucial matters of the soul that Christmas is meant to inspire. This week, focus on being fully present in your spiritual reflection.

Date: _____

Week 51

Be a relentless force of hope.

B.R.E.W. Starter: In her award-winning short story "Soon," Pam Durban writes about the life of Martha Crawford. Martha dreams, wishes, and plans, but life doesn't work out quite like she expects. Yet she keeps on keeping on, resisting the temptation to become frigid to life. Something keeps welling up inside of Martha: hope, a force "so necessary to survival in this world, that you were not just trudging along but moving *toward* something."[7]

Ask loved ones about their four or five biggest hopes for the coming year. List your own smallest and grandest hopes.

---

7. The Best American Short Stories, 1997, *ed. E. Anne Proulx (Boston: Houghton Mifflin, 1997), 263.*

Date: _____

Week 52

You have the last word.

B.R.E.W. Starter: This week, write your own B.R.E.W. thought starter. Remember, you do have the last word. Though circumstances and influences fill our world, ultimately we decide on what we will believe and how we will live our lives. Our freedom to choose in this way is God's greatest gift to us. I hope you choose to learn and grow in marvelous new ways each day. I hope you choose hope and laughter. I hope you choose and keep on choosing joy. Now, make the last word yours.

B.R.E.W. ONLINE

Visit www.brewseries.com to read weekly B.R.E.W. inspirations from Kirk Byron Jones as well as B.R.E.W. testimonies and suggestions from readers. The site will also be your most up-to-date resource for forthcoming B.R.E.W. books, workbooks, audios, and other exciting and practical creations in the B.R.E.W. series.

About the Author

Dr. Jones currently teaches ethics and preaching at Andover Newton Theological School, and serves as a guest preacher and teacher at churches, schools, and conferences throughout the United States. His writings have been published in various journals, including *Leadership, Gospel Today, Pulpit Digest*, and *The African American Pulpit*, a quarterly preaching journal he co-founded in 1997.

Reverend Jones is the creator of an inspirational card collection called *Savoring Pace Life Lines* and www.savoringpace.com, a Web site which offers weekly reflections on cherishing life in a rushing world.

Dr. Jones is the author of *Rest in the Storm: Self-Care Strategies for Clergy and Other Caregivers* and *Addicted to Hurry: Spiritual Strategies for Slowing Down*, both published by Judson Press, and *The Jazz of Preaching: How to Preach with Great Freedom and Joy*, published by Abingdon Press.

You may learn more about Dr. Jones's speaking and writing at www.kirkbjones.com.

Look Your Troubles in the Face Until They Soften and Teach You Something

Psalm 23:4

Problems Are Opportunities in Disguise

2 Corinthians 3:8-9

Choose JOY

John 15:4

You Were Born to Play and Soar

Isaiah 40:31

morning
B.R.E.W.
A Divine Power Drink for Your Soul

Be Still
Receive God's Love
Embrace Personhood
Welcome the Day

To order the book and
journal containing these
empowerment cards visit
www.augsburgfortress.org

---

morning
B.R.E.W.
A Divine Power Drink for Your Soul

Be Still
Receive God's Love
Embrace Personhood
Welcome the Day

To order the book and
journal containing these
empowerment cards visit
www.augsburgfortress.org

---

morning
B.R.E.W.
A Divine Power Drink for Your Soul

Be Still
Receive God's Love
Embrace Personhood
Welcome the Day

To order the book and
journal containing these
empowerment cards visit
www.augsburgfortress.org

---

morning
B.R.E.W.
A Divine Power Drink for Your Soul

Be Still
Receive God's Love
Embrace Personhood
Welcome the Day

To order the book and
journal containing these
empowerment cards visit
www.augsburgfortress.org

Greatness
Is Your
Birthright
Psalm 8:4-5

Without the
Rest,
There Is No
MUSIC
Matthew 11:28

Stand
Strong
in God's
Love
John 3:16

Play Your
SONG
Psalm 96:1

Be Still

Receive God's Love

Embrace Personhood

Welcome the Day

To order the book and
journal containing these
empowerment cards visit
www.augsburgfortress.org

m o r n i n g

B.R.E.W.

A Divine Power Drink for Your Soul

Be Still

Receive God's Love

Embrace Personhood

Welcome the Day

To order the book and
journal containing these
empowerment cards visit
www.augsburgfortress.org

m o r n i n g

B.R.E.W.

A Divine Power Drink for Your Soul

Be Still

Receive God's Love

Embrace Personhood

Welcome the Day

To order the book and
journal containing these
empowerment cards visit
www.augsburgfortress.org

m o r n i n g

B.R.E.W.

A Divine Power Drink for Your Soul

Be Still

Receive God's Love

Embrace Personhood

Welcome the Day

To order the book and
journal containing these
empowerment cards visit
www.augsburgfortress.org